OUR NEST
in the
UNIVERSE

Poems, Essays, and Short Stories
of a Year in Northern Michigan

Jeffrey K. Leestma

MISSION POINT PRESS

Published by Mission Point Press
2554 Chandler Rd.
Traverse City, MI 49696
(231) 421-9513
www.MissionPointPress.com

Hardcover ISBN: 978-1-961302-65-5
Softcover ISBN: 978-1-961302-87-7

Library of Congress Control Number is available upon request.

Printed in the United States of America

For Tracy, Kirsten and Hanna

Contents

Introduction

My wife, Tracy, and I, along with our German shepherd, Finn, moved to Emmet County in Northern Michigan in the fall of 2022. We were not strangers to the area, having visited there often over the decades. I spent much of my high school and college years at Pickerel Lake, where my parents owned a year-round cottage for many years.

The house we recently purchased is in the woods, nestled among maples and oaks and poplars, with a smattering of white pines and spruce trees for contrast. It is much different than the suburban life we had just left. It gave us a new perspective, living among the trees and a wide variety of critters. So, I decided to write about our first year in our new home.

I realize that I am far from being the first to write about the changing seasons in Northern Michigan. In fact, it has been done so often that it's almost a genre in itself.

My idea was that I would write about our experience in Northern Michigan in creative verse. Poetry, mainly, peppered with some essays and a few short stories, as well as a few thought pieces.

But even though this is mainly poetry, it's based on facts and real observations. If I write about an opossum crossing our yard in broad daylight, it really happened. The short stories, though fictional, are based on historical facts.

And I wanted this to be an easy read, even lighthearted, and at times humorous. So, while this will be a quick read, my sincere hope is that you simply find it enjoyable. I hope this book earns a permanent place on the bookshelf of your cottage or cabin, and that you are inclined to return to it time and again.

FINN IN OUR WOODS

Two Deer in the Woods

I took Finn out, at dawn, to do her thing.
And at once, her nose caught a scent a-wing.

Through the bare trees I saw a buck, out a stone's throw,
And then slightly behind it, not surprisingly, a doe.

Silhouettes they were, with nary a twitch,
The hair on Finn's back at a vertical pitch.

I told Finn to stay, and she rightly obeyed,
And the buck and the doe, they similarly stayed.

It was a showdown of sorts to see who would move first,
All I could think of were scenarios worst.

The doe was the first to break the tension,
Finn's fur remained, still, at upright attention.

The buck was next, and bolted off with a rush,
And no longer could they be seen through the thick of the brush.

The standoff was over, tranquility secured,
And Finn finished her business as if nothing occurred.

January 2

Good Morning!

I rose to a morning still and dark,
And a farm dog's far-off distant bark.
Was it a very important barnyard warning?
Or just a dog simply wishing the world "Good Morning!"

January 4

A Solo Performance

A fox came to visit us last night.
A cautious and skitterish fella,
It danced on our lawn,
To left and to right,
All by itself, *a cappella*.

January 8

STUBBORN OAK

The Stubborn Oak

I'm looking out the back window into the woods.

On the edge of the snow-covered lawn, where the woods begin, stands an oak tree. In the lifespan of oak trees, this one is a youngster, maybe twenty years old with a trunk only about a foot or so in diameter at the base.

I would not call this a stately oak. When it comes to oak trees, the word "stately" is often reserved for trees that are perhaps a half-century old or older. An oak that you can safely hang a tire swing from. An oak that provides broad, cooling shade for a large summer picnic.

This is not that kind of oak tree.

But what this oak tree lacks in "stateliness," it more than makes up for in stubbornness. You see, this is January in Northern Michigan. The temperatures are often in the single digits. Yet this oak is still holding on to about a quarter of its leaves, leaves that stubbornly resisted falling to earth in October along with the rest of the leaf-shedding tree universe.

The leaves are brown and brittle, just like the ones you'd rake up off the ground in autumn, yet they continue to hang on. When the wind blows, they make a crinkled-paper sound that cuts through the silence of a snow-covered winter, stubbornly thumbing their noses at the other trees in the forest that gave up on summer without a fight.

I'm quite sure that there is a scientific explanation for this phenomenon, but I want no part of it. I'll just continue to enjoy their tenacity and simply wait until spring, when the new generation of green leaves push them, finally, into retirement.

January 17

WINTER BIRCH

Winter Birch

silvery fingers
hardened branches reach naked
against a grey sky

January 18

HEAVY SNOW

A Quilt of Snow

We got about eight inches of snow yesterday and overnight. Whoever coined the phrase "blanket of snow" pretty much got it right.

Yesterday's snow was not of the cold, powdery variety. No, this snow was wet, so it is sticking, heavy, everywhere, more like how shaving cream sticks to a face. The wet snow is weighing down branches, taking some of the cedar and pine boughs almost to the ground. The northwest edges of the tree trunks in the woods are covered with snow, indicating the direction from which the snowstorm came.

Yes, this is a blanket of snow, but as I look out the back window it somehow looks more like a quilt than a blanket. Over the snow-white canvas of my view, I can see the gray-green needles of the pine, the stubborn brown leaves hanging on to the oak, the ornamental grasses now turned beige, the red-roofed birdhouse on a wooden post, and the pattern of the snow-topped firewood stacked near "the barn," our garage at the back of the property. I can see footprints in the snow, made by both man and beast.

January 20

Critter Highway

Footprints across our snowy yard
From trees, over lawn, to trees.
A snow-printed boulevard
Made by critter expertise.

A 'possum was the first to go,
Its tail signature expertly penned.
Then, a raccoon meandered to and fro,
On the tail-end highway of his 'possum friend.

Last night a skunk ventured through,
Its aroma bitter cayenne.
Spoiled woodside avenue,
Never to be used again.

February 1

Groundhog Day

The groundhog shadow he sees is
The source of annual teases.
It really does not matter,
The rodent pig's chatter,
Winter does as she dad-gum well pleases!

February 2

Wishing to Go Fishing

I'm longing to fish on the ice,
With an auger and angling device.
But a frostbitten nose,
And icicle toes,
Give me good reason to think twice.

February 15

A Hint of Spring

snow still covers ground
clear topaz blue skies above
distant woodpecker

March 6

A 'Possum Crossed the Yard

A 'possum crossed the yard this afternoon.
Does it not know it is nocturnal?
Perhaps it was a trial balloon,
To alter its 'possum clock internal.

It strutted with a most confident jaunt,
A downright forest socialite.
Chic, arrogant and nonchalant.
Just too *haute* to save for the night.

March 6

Northern Lights

Magnetosphere and solar winds;
Optical wavelength calamity.
Thermospheric spectral emissions;
Polar electrochemistry.

Particles charged and ionic rays;
Electrons and protons that cross and that criss,
An atmospheric bouillabaisse.
Aurora borealis.

March 23

Winter Fights Back

Yesterday Spring said, "I'm here at last!"
Today Winter said, "Not so fast."
Yesterday was blue skies and finches.
Today brought eight white inches.

Yesterday Spring said, "It's time to celebrate!"
Today Winter said, "You'll just have to wait."
Yesterday boasted a slightly warmer breeze.
Today Winter brought Spring to its knees.

March 25

The First Sign of Spring

The first sign of spring is not what you think.
Not the arrival of warm blue skies,
Nor snow piles beginning to shrink.
It's when the fishers retreat from the ice.

Not when the robin finds its first worm,
Nor April rains from which flowers arise,
Nor tulips beginning to form.
It's when the fishers retreat from the ice.

Not when icicles drip from the eaves,
Nor when a tailed kite flies,
Nor when tree buds hope to become leaves.
It's when the fishers retreat from the ice.

March 28

Delayed Again

I thought spring had arrived, I truly did.
On Friday, a folding chair and a little kickback.
On Saturday, snow again, I do not kid.
Two steps forward, one step back.

Spring is coming, I just feel it.
I long for summer's sweet soundtrack,
But nature hesitates to reveal it.
Two steps forward, one step back.

April 8

A Day of Firsts

It snowed here a few days ago. Yet today, it reached seventy-two degrees. It was as if we skipped spring completely and went straight to summer. Warm wind. Blue skies.

Spring and autumn are shorter in Northern Michigan than in lower Michigan. Up north, in April, snow can hang around through the month, but once May arrives, the warmth comes as surely as the tourists and the fudge. Similarly, summer can last through October, but once November arrives, winter clenches its icy fist.

But today, in April, summer pushed spring out of the way and said to winter, "Enough is enough!"

Today, I saw the season's first housefly.

Today, I saw the first boat moored at the marina.

Today, I pulled the chaise lounge from the barn, rolled up my pant legs and the sleeves of my shirt, and took a barefoot nap in the sun.

April 10

A Lonely Song Heard in the Woods

lonely mourning dove
why does it wail so sadly?
boo-HOO woo woo woo

April 11

The Snow Is Melting
Faster Now

The snow is melting faster now.
The earth is beginning to show itself again in big patches.
The ice is melting on the pond, particularly closer to shore,
Where the water is warmer.
Snow is gone from the branches.
Snow is gone from the rooftops.
The snow is melting faster now.

April 12

NEST EGGS

Spring!

All of the senses are subdued in winter. In winter, colors are grays and whites, except for those rare, clear winter days when the sun shines and the skies are so blue you have to squint to look heavenward. In winter, there is deafening silence, broken only by an occasional mourning dove, or a crow, or a distant dog barking, or the wind through the pines.

Spring! Spring brings with it greens and yellows and reds. Spring brings the smell of damp soil and new growth, and the sappy aroma of pine boughs. Spring brings the sounds of waves lapping the shore, laughing children, a bullfrog or two, and the sweet sounds of birds who made the long trip up from warmer climates, unpacked their bags, and announced, "We're back for the season, and it's great to see you again!"

April 18

Tug O' War

Winter on this side, summer away,
A back-and-forth warm-cold ballet,
With spring in the middle
Inching little by little,
Toward the sweetest embrace of May.

April 18

Shadow Figure

Our resident little red fox,
His behavior unorthodox.
He stays in the shadows,
Wherever he goes,
When he's out for one of his walks.

April 22

SPRUCE

Spring Rain

in the thick grey mist
raindrops cling to pine needles
like crystal jewels

April 25

THE MIGHTY MAC

Bridges

Saturday, May 3, 1952
The Cocktail Lounge, The Hotel Perry, Petoskey, Michigan

Two men were seated at the bar. One of them was smoking a cigarette and he would occasionally tap the ashes into a glass ashtray. It was a small bar, just four stools across. The bar was at the short end of a long room, which was partially below the sidewalk level just outside the door. One of the long walls was of brick, and the opposite long wall was clad in knotty pine. The room contained small square tables, each topped with a clean, clear glass ashtray. Behind the bar was a cash register surrounded by bottles of liquor and more knotty pine.

The man with the cigarette sat on the stool to the right, and he sat in such a way that he was slightly leaning against the brick wall. He wore a tidy blue plaid shirt tucked neatly into gray wool pants. The other man sat on the stool second from the left, so that there was just one empty stool between them. He wore a dark blue suit and tie and a gray fedora sat atop the bar. The man in the suit looked to be in his early thirties and a little out of place wearing a suit on a Saturday. The man in the plaid shirt was perhaps ten years older. Other than the two men, the lounge was empty.

The bartender soon returned to the bar, by way of a swinging half-door to the left of the bar. He took the man's ashtray and placed it underneath the bar and replaced it with a clean one. "Can I offer you gentlemen a cold beer?" he asked.

"Sure," they both said.

The bartender wore a white shirt and a thin striped tie. His sleeves were rolled up to just below the elbow. He grabbed two glasses, held them up to the light, wiped them with his apron, held them up to the light again, and then placed the empty glasses in front of the men. He pulled two bottles of beer from the cooler, opened them with a bottle opener, and poured both beers at the same time, one in each hand, and placed the half-empty bottles next to the glasses.

"The weather is starting to get warmer," the man with the cigarette said. "Won't be long before the summer folks begin to arrive."

"And none too soon," replied the bartender. "Beginning in June, the hotel is booked through the summer, which means this place gets real busy. I'm already hiring help for the summer months, you know, waiters and waitresses. Mostly college kids."

The man in the plaid shirt and cigarette turned to the man next to him and said, "I don't believe I've seen you here before. Are you new in town?"

"I'm here on business," the man replied. "I'm staying at the hotel."

Both men took a swallow of beer. The man in the suit then turned to the other and said, "What do you do for a living, if I may ask?"

"I'm in real estate," he answered.

"How is that going for you?"

"I do okay. Petoskey has been a summer resort area for a hundred years. People used to come by train, or by boat from Chicago or Milwaukee. Now it's all about the automobile, and since the war ended, we see new faces up here all the time. It's more than just tourism now. Now people want to live here rather than just visit. It's still mostly summer tourists, but about three years ago, they opened up a ski hill south of here in Boyne Falls."

"A ski hill? Really?"

"Yes. I'm still not convinced that it's not just a passing fad, but it is attracting people from Detroit, Lansing, and Grand Rapids during the winter months. That can only spell good things for the real estate business. It's all about sales and rentals." There was a brief pause. "And what do you do?"

"I'm in sales too. I sell electric typewriters. I actually come here quite often. Northern Michigan is my territory."

"And how is that working out?"

"We can't keep pace with demand. I mean, once a secretary tries out an electric typewriter, I can't fill out the order fast enough. And the best thing about it is that electric typewriters will be here forever. Once a thing is electrified, it's as good as it's going to get. A hundred years from now, people will still be using electric typewriters."

"Sounds like you have a license to print money with that product."

"It's kind of like that. Every business has manual typewriters, right? On Monday I have an appointment with the local newspaper. They must have a dozen or more typewriters!"

"Yes, I guess you're right."

The men sat quietly for a few minutes, tending to their beers.

The bartender broke the silence. "Say, did you hear that Lansing gave the go-ahead a few days ago to build a bridge connecting the Upper and Lower Peninsulas? They're selling bonds worth 85 million dollars to start construction."

"Yes, I did read about it in the paper," the real estate agent said. "It has taken decades to get to this point. Now, we will finally have a connected state."

"Yes, I heard about it too," said the man in the suit. "Personally, I think they ought to leave well enough alone. I mean, really, a five-mile-long bridge? Is that even possible? Why don't they send a man to the moon while they're at it?"

"I don't know," said the man in plaid. "I kind of like the idea that I can drive to the U.P. any time I want, and I don't have to wait hours for the ferry. Plus, just imagine all the real estate that will open up."

"Well, that might work for you, but the farther north I go, the fewer electric typewriters I sell. I work on volume. If someone up there wants an electric typewriter, they can order one from Sears Roebuck or Montgomery Ward."

"I guess you're right. But, you know, people in St. Ignace, Sault Ste. Marie, Marquette, Houghton, and a lot of other places up there use typewriters. You might be missing out on a big opportunity."

"Well, maybe. But I live downstate, and it just takes too much time to get there, even when, or if, this newfangled Mackinac Bridge gets built."

"Yes, I guess you're right. But the new bridge is going to make the

Upper Peninsula more accessible to everyone. And the new bridge is also going to give Michigan residents in the U.P. easier access to things and opportunities down here. Imagine all the trucks carrying goods going back and forth. And tourists! A bridge can be a lot more than concrete, steel girders and cable, you know. A bridge can bring people together. In this case, our fellow Michiganians."

The men each ordered another beer and sat in silence.

The real estate agent spoke first. "You know, it's not the first time there has been a bridge across the straits."

"What do you mean?"

"There have been winters so cold that the water freezes solid, and people and animals can cross back and forth over the ice. It's quite common to get to Mackinac Island from St. Ignace in the winter simply by crossing the ice. And I'm pretty sure an ice bridge is how wolves and moose first got to Isle Royale. Bridges, even ice bridges, have a way of connecting things and leveling things."

Again, silence.

"You've heard the phrase 'I'll cross that bridge when I come to it,'" said the real estate man.

"Of course."

"It means putting something off until you can't put it off any longer. I feel that the Mackinac Bridge is a literal bridge that can't be put off any longer. The increase in tourists and automobiles has made ferries obsolete. Imagine that you are a family on vacation, with your wife and kids, and you just spent five hours getting to Mackinaw City. Do you really want to wait another two or three or four hours waiting to drive your car on the ferry? Then, it takes another hour to cross the straits and get your car unloaded. Crossing a five-mile-long bridge at sixty miles per hour would take about five minutes."

"Yes, but I honestly don't think a bridge that big can be built. It's impossible! And at what cost?"

"I understand what you're saying. It's going to be a big bridge. But just think how proud all of us in Michigan will be to boast that we have the longest suspension bridge in the world!"

"I suppose."

"There's a great quote from Henry David Thoreau about bridges. I can't recite it word for word, but, basically, he said that a kid can gather the materials to build a bridge to the moon, but a middle-aged man will build a shed with them."

"I get it. It takes courage to dream big."

"It does. There's another adage that says don't burn your bridges. It means doing something in a way that you can never return. It means that you've forever broken ties with something or someone. The opposite of that is to build bridges, to forge ties and build relationships."

After about five minutes the real estate agent said, "Say, when you're up here selling electric typewriters, do you ever take the time to look out over Little Traverse Bay? Have you taken the time to take in one of our sunsets?"

"What do you mean?"

"I mean, do you ever take the time to notice how beautiful it is up here in Northern Michigan?"

"I do. It really is beautiful up here. I think this would be a great place to retire."

There was pause. The real estate agent in the blue plaid shirt spoke again. "Why wait? You won't retire for another thirty years. You know, traveling to your sales territory would be a whole lot easier if you actually lived in your sales territory. I've got something I'd like you to see."

He reached down to a leather briefcase leaning against the stool and pulled out a manila envelope. He slid over to the next bar stool, bridging the gap between them.

"I want you to take a look at a piece of property." He pulled several black and white glossy photos from the envelope. "This is a place on Douglas Lake. A hundred feet of frontage on the water. Sandy beach. It's a summer place now but could easily be converted to a year-round home. It's halfway between Petoskey and that new bridge, and all those customers in the Upper Peninsula."

"This is beautiful," the salesman said. "I just don't know."

"I know it's a little pricey, about eight thousand dollars. But believe me when I tell you that you can't go wrong here. It will always increase in value. You won't regret it."

"I just don't know. Eight thousand dollars is more than I paid for my house downstate. I'll need to discuss it with my wife."

"Of course. Take these photos with you. Here's my business card. But don't wait too long."

"Okay, I won't. Hey, thanks!"

"Sure."

There was silence again.

"Hey, can I buy you another beer?" asked the man in the suit.

"Okay, just one more."

The bartender poured two more beers into two clean glasses.

"Cheers."

"Cheers."

"By the way," said the real estate man in the blue plaid shirt. "I have three old typewriters in my office."

This is a fictional story, but the facts are accurate. The Mackinac Bridge, "the Mighty Mac," was indeed the world's longest suspension bridge in the world when it opened in 1957. It has since been surpassed, but it still ranks among the longest bridges in the world. Today it stands as one of the world's most impressive and enduring engineering marvels and is a proud symbol of the State of Michigan. It is undoubtedly one of the best investments made by the state, linking in a very physical way the Upper and Lower Peninsulas. The Hotel Perry still stands proudly today, now known as the Perry Hotel, and during the '60s, '70s and '80s it was known as the Perry-Davis Hotel. The Lounge has been refurbished and is now called the Noggin Room, a favorite hangout for locals and tourists alike.

Fire Pit

season's first campfire
lit from old dry stacked wood and
winter forest twigs

May 6

The Last Flight

Yesterday I took my last airline flight.

And the reason I can almost assuredly say that is because we've found our nest in the universe. Our place on earth. Our one-and-a-half acre, wooded, critter inhabited, peaceful nest in the universe in Northern Michigan. No need to travel now except by automobile or train.

But I got to thinking about that flight, and how that plane was a lot like life, but on a smaller scale; a microcosm of life on earth. And of faith.

You see, I couldn't see the Pilot as I boarded the plane. The cockpit door was closed. But I had faith that the Pilot was in there, and I put my faith in the Pilot that He would get me to my destination.

I looked at the people on the plane with me. People of different genders, ages, and races. Some nice people. Some, not so nice. Wealthy. Poor. Kind. Rude. Healthy. Sick. Some wanted to talk; others kept to themselves.

I realized that at some point, everyone on that plane had to get along, or at least endure each other, until the flight ended.

We all had to share the same space. There was a limited amount of food and water and it had to be shared among all the passengers. We were all breathing the same air.

And when we safely reached our destination, there was the Pilot, standing at the cockpit door, saying, "Welcome home!"

May 13

New Growth

tender fresh leaves of
maple, birch, oak and popple,
green springtime morning

May 14

Trillium

white on edge of woods
so tired of hibernating
coming up for air

May 15

The First Sign of Summer

The first sign of summer is not what you think.
Not when crickets at night keep you awake,
Nor the sweet iced tea that you drink.
It's when laughter returns to the lake.

Not when cornfields are turned over,
Nor a pink sunburn ache,
Nor when bees converse with the clover.
It's when laughter returns to the lake.

Not the red-winged blackbird's grudge,
Nor the sizzle of a backyard steak,
Nor the welcomed return of tourist fudge.
It's when laughter returns to the lake.

May 20

Sparrows & Finches

Sparrows and finches are happy ol' fellas,
Dressed in browns and sometimes in yellas.
And in the case of rain,
They rarely complain,
They use maples and oaks as umbrellas.

May 22

Whirligigs

like helicopters
tiny maple seedlings fly
drifting from heaven

May 22

FOREST FLOOR

Morel Hunting

There are mushrooms growing at the edge of the woods
But they are clearly of the poisonous kind.

Still, might it not be a good idea
To see if there are some morels out there to find.

Morels, you see, are quite delicious,
Sought for recipes both simple and refined.

So, I grabbed a sack and my pocketknife
With thoughts of good eatin' on my mind.

I traversed the woods, back and forth,
Not an inch of soil did I leave unmined.

But not a single morel was found today,
Dashed were my hopes of fine dinners dined.

So, for now, every one of my morel-themed dishes
Will include mushrooms of the grocery store kind.

May 23

The Fishfly

I found a fishfly on the porch railing today.
How it got there it's not easy to say.

You see, we're about a half-mile from the river source;
Fishflies simply don't fly that far, of course.

And between here and there is mostly wood,
Which would hinder the fish-flight, even if it could.

Did the fishfly, perhaps by bird, arrive?
Unlikely, though, because it was very much alive.

Or perhaps by the wind, on a fantastical sail,
Placing it ever-so-gently on our front porch rail.

The answer is somewhat less adventurous I feel.
It most likely thumbed a ride on an automobile!

May 23

Fox Family

Our resident foxes now count four,
Mama fox, Papa fox and now two more.
Mama babysits,
Her two baby kits,
An instinctive maternal chore.

The kits bound at night o'er the yard,
Mama is always on guard.
She teaches them tricks,
Like fox politics,
The matriarch *très avant-garde*.

Papa fox, it's worth to state,
His occupation, to propagate.
He'll hunt for food,
For his growing brood,
While tracking the fertility rate.

May 24

Japanese Rain

Rain is different in Japan.
Born of the sea.
Held close in the mountains.
Nearer to earth, so it lands softly.

A gentle rain. A deliberate rain.

Raindrops fall with a slower cadence.
Tapping curiously on the windowsill.
Holding tightly to pine needles and gutters.
Dancing politely in puddles.

A calm rain. A kind rain.

Today, Japanese rain visited our woods.

June 14

Longest Day of the Year

Summer solstice is what they name it,
Not so easy, however, to explain it.

The earth tilts in such a way,
That the sun is highest at midday.

The sun aligns with the Tropic of Cancer,
But for me that is just half the answer.

The sun is twenty-three degrees north of the equator,
Which means I'll enjoy my summer day later.

June 21

FINN IN LITTLE TRAVERSE BAY

Summer

Nests in trees
Sunburned knees
Buzzing bees
Dogs with fleas

Water skis
Pollen sneeze
Lakeside breeze
Cotton tees

Cottage cheese
Inland seas
Life of ease
Ice cream freeze

Tire trapeze
Golfing fees
Early peas
Sweet corn please!

June 25

Summer Perfection

Today is the perfect summer day. About ninety degrees Fahrenheit. Sunny. Still. Quiet.

A passing car kicks up dry dust that lingers in the air and fills the nose.

Too hot for mosquitoes. Most birds have taken refuge beneath shady branches. Bumblebees and deerflies are not deterred by the heat. Nor is the occasional white cabbage butterfly. The air is filled with the warm fragrance of tomato plants and marigolds.

This is a day to take a folding lawn chair and seek the coolness of a shade tree. Or relax on a screened porch positioned on the shady side of the house. A slight breeze, when there is one, washes over you like a damp cloth.

Loose-fitting clothes. Cool buttoned shirts. Breezy cotton dresses. Bare feet.

Tea or lemonade poured over ice in tall glasses. Quiet conversations, as if speaking softly will keep you cooler.

Those who seek "comfort" in air-conditioned confinement will never know the pleasure of a perfect summer day.

July 4

Herb Garden

watching basil grow
rosemary, oregano
chives by my window

July 16

"PEACEFUL WATERS"

Peaceful Waters

I spent the better part of today on the Northern Arrow of the Grand Rapids & Indiana Railway, now a part of the Pennsylvania line, and I arrived in Petoskey early this evening. My destination: the Pon-She-Wa-Ing Hotel, on the shores of Crooked Lake in Ponshewaing, Michigan, about ten miles northeast of Petoskey, to relax and do some fishing.

The Northern Arrow made prolonged stops today at Kalamazoo, Grand Rapids and Cadillac, not to mention the dozens of smaller stops depending on passenger destinations. We stopped at Walton, Michigan, not at all a big town, a village really, to allow passengers to deboard to catch the next train toward Traverse City. The spur breaks away just north of Walton and goes not only to Traverse City, but all the way to Northport in the Leelanau Peninsula.

In years past, I could have arrived in Petoskey and transferred to a local commuter train, also known as a dummy train, and taken it to the Alanson station, just a mile or two north of Ponshewaing. Some dummies would have even dropped me off at a flag stop in Ponshewaing, consisting of just a couple of trackside benches, but conveniently located right across the road from the Pon-She-Wa-Ing Hotel.

But this is 1949, and the dummies are long gone. Dummy service ended around 1925. I hired a driver to take me the ten miles to the hotel.

It was a beautiful drive on U.S. 31 north out of Petoskey. As we drove through Bay View, an old summer community of Victorian cottages, the sun was setting over Little Traverse Bay, painting the sky with varying hues of oranges and blues. On the hill just south of the village of Conway, I caught my first glimpse of Crooked Lake. It was then that I knew that Ponshewaing was just minutes away.

We pulled off U.S. 31 into the entrance of the Pon-She-Wa-Ing Hotel, passing between two stone pillars on either side of the sandy driveway. As we approached the hotel, the warm light from the windows and the front porch made the journey seem all worthwhile. Fireflies were everywhere.

Even in the dusk, I noticed the number of cars parked just off the drive. Before the war, almost all guests arrived by train, but now, the automobile seems to be the better way to travel. Station wagons and large sedans lined the drive.

My driver pulled up in front of the hotel, and I began to unload my luggage and my fishing gear from the trunk. "Good evening! We've been expecting you!" bellowed the proprietor from the front porch. "The dining room is closed for the night," he said, "but I saved a plate for you. Fried bluegill, tomato and cottage cheese salad, and carrots and peas. I hope that's okay."

"Sounds delicious," I answered. "I'm hungry."

"Great," he said. "I also saved you a slice of cherry pie. The tart cherries are in season, and we just got a bushel delivered from Traverse City yesterday. The missus made the pies just this morning."

"Are the fish biting?" I asked.

"Yes," he answered, "but the water is getting warm, so you need to fish deep. Crooked Lake is shallow, so I suggest you head over to Pickerel Lake. You'll need to get up early, so let's get you fed and settled in for the night."

Journal, Saturday, July 16, 1949

I woke to the ringing of my alarm clock. Five thirty. I turned it off as quickly as possible so as not to disturb the other guests. The walls are thin in this old house.

I threw on my dungarees, an undershirt, and a wool plaid shirt over that. It wouldn't be long before the wool shirt would come off, but it helped with the early morning chill.

I headed downstairs. I knew I wouldn't be the only fisherman heading out this morning, but so far, I was the only person moving. The stairs took me to the living room, with its pinewood floors, brick fireplace with a stuffed northern pike hanging over the mantel, and plenty of wicker furniture.

Being July, the windows were left open all night, and the morning breeze lent a certain freshness to the musty smell that never really seems to go away in an old structure, particularly one that is closed up all winter.

The Pon-She-Wa-Ing Hotel is not a hotel in the normal sense. It's more like an oversized house or cottage. It was built around the turn of the century on old Native American grounds. The current owners have managed the hotel almost from the beginning.

The two-story house is designed so that the floor plan is like a giant "H" – two gabled wings at each end that are connected in the middle. Wide porches span both the front and back. The clapboards are painted a fresh white, which also serves as a beacon of sorts when returning from the lake late in the evening.

There is a boathouse on the property, as well as a barn and a woodshop. There is also a nice sized garden, where the owners grow many of their summer vegetables, and a round, man-made "trout pond" situated halfway between the house and the shore.

The first floor is devoted primarily to living and dining, as well as the owner's quarters. Guest rooms are upstairs.

In the other direction from the stairs is the dining room, consisting of about ten square tables and slat-backed wooden chairs. It was empty now, but the tables were already dressed in tablecloths, with plates, silverware and glasses waiting for breakfast guests on a buffet table. Breakfast wouldn't be served until seven o'clock.

I heard some banging in the kitchen, not to mention the aroma of bacon, so I headed that way. There, I found the cook, Billy, already preparing for the morning guests.

"Good morning, sir," he said when he saw me standing in the kitchen doorway. "Heading out on the lake?"

"That I am," I answered. "Any chance I can get a cup of coffee?"

"Absolutely," he said. "Grab a cup over there and help yourself. Breakfast isn't ready yet, but there's a bowl and some corn flakes over there. Milk is in the ice box. Oh, and grab a few slices of bacon. The bacon is under that towel staying warm."

"Thank you so much," I said.

I stood at the countertop, trying my best to stay out of the way, eating my corn flakes and crispy bacon, and washing it all down with coffee fresh out of the urn.

"I'll tell you what," he added. "It's too early to start on the eggs, so how about I pack you a lunch for the water?"

"You don't have to do that," I protested.

"It's really no problem at all. Is a ham and cheese sandwich okay?"

"That would be great. Thank you."

Billy cut the sandwich in half and wrapped it in wax paper. Then he placed it in a brown paper bag along with an apple and some fresh Traverse City cherries. "Here you go," he said, handing me the bag. "Don't forget to take a canteen of water with you."

"Where are you keeping the nightcrawlers these days?" I asked.

"I believe they're in a metal cooler next to the boathouse door. If you don't see them, come get me and we'll look around."

"Thanks, Billy." I grabbed my rod and reel and my tackle box and headed outside. By now, a few more fishermen were stirring inside the house, their footsteps could be heard on the wood floors above. I walked to the boat house, and just like Billy said, there was a cooler filled with waxy paper cottage cheese cartons. Inside each carton was some moist moss and dirt and a good number of wriggling worms.

I walked out on the dock and placed my gear in an old wooden boat, maybe ten feet long, with a greenish-silver, 10-horsepower Johnson Sea-Horse outboard motor at the stern. The motor looked fairly new, with maybe only one full season behind it. I shook the gas can. Full.

There was a little bit of standing water on the floor of the boat that collected seaweed, old bait, silvery fish scales, and white paint flakes. I was pretty sure that the water would evaporate by mid-morning.

On each side of the bow, the name "Topinabee" was stenciled in faded, flaky blue paint, a wink of an eye to the old double-decker, open-air steamer of the same name that used to sail the inland waterway from Oden on Crooked Lake, through Burt Lake to Mullet Lake and on to Cheboygan. The Topinabee, named after Chief Topinabee, would sometimes even sail to Mackinac Island and Sault Ste. Marie.

Finally settled, I pulled the choke on the motor, and after the third pull of the starter cord, the Johnson came to life. I unwound the line from the cleats on the dock, first in the front, and then the rear, and pushed off. The sky was getting lighter in the east, and the birds were getting down to brass tacks.

I was glad that I had my own boat and motor. In the old days, a steam-powered "launch" would tow multiple boats out in the lake and drop them off at various fishing holes. The boats were equipped only with a pair of oars and an anchor. At the end of the day, the launch would collect all the boats and tow them back to the hotel.

The hotel is on the north side of the lake, and I headed south toward the river that connects Crooked Lake with Pickerel Lake. Halfway in, there is a very deep small pond called the Black Hole. I dropped anchor and was surprised how far it sank before hitting bottom.

The sky was turning blue, and I could see the sun hitting the treetops across from me, but I was still in the shade. The mosquitoes were as thick as thieves. I was glad that I was wearing my wool shirt, and I tied a bandana around my neck.

I opened my tackle box and reached for a silver spinner, hoping that it would reflect enough light to get the attention of a big fish. After numerous casts and nothing to show for it, I decided to go with a sure thing: worms.

I have a few artificial lures in my tackle box, but I have always found that live bait works best: nightcrawlers, minnows, crickets. I grabbed the cottage cheese carton and dug around for a worm. I pinched off a one-inch piece of worm and threaded it onto a hook. About four feet up the line from the hook I attached a red and white wooden bobber.

I cast the line about ten feet offshore, next to a tree branch that was sticking out of the water, and I let the worm do its work.

Bingo! Almost immediately I felt a tug and the bobber disappeared under water. Based on the fight this fish was giving me, I presumed it to be a bass rather than a bluegill or crappie. The fish took my line, bobber and all, and swam underneath and around the sunken tree branch.

Afraid that the branch was going to cut my line, I relaxed the tension, hoping the fish would take a rest. I was trying to figure out my next move, when the fish slowly moved backwards, either on its own or because of the current, and moved around the tree, backtracking the way it got in. Now free of the branch, the fish darted, fast and deep toward the center of the Black Hole. I pulled back and reeled, pulled back and reeled, afraid of letting the fish get too far away and getting tangled in whatever might be lurking in the depths of the pond.

I kept reeling until finally, the fish offered little resistance. I had tuckered the big boy out, and when I pulled him into the boat with a net, I got my first glimpse of my prize, a 16-inch largemouth bass, easily big enough to be a "keeper" yet not big enough to pay a visit to the local taxidermist. I removed the hook and clipped the fish to a stringer and dropped it back in the water for safekeeping. The other end of the stringer was securely tied to a cleat inside the boat.

I had a pretty good morning in the Black Hole, catching a half-dozen bluegills and another bass, which I let go because it had some more growing to do.

Around eleven o'clock, I removed my wool shirt, and motored into Pickerel Lake far enough from shore so the mosquitoes would leave me alone, set myself adrift unanchored, and thoroughly enjoyed Billy's packed lunch and the sun on my face.

I fished a bit more after lunch, catching a few more bluegills and another nice bass, this time a smallmouth. Since I had floated down most of the length of Pickerel Lake, I decided to fire up the Johnson and circle the lake before heading back to the hotel.

I noticed that the water in the bottom of the boat had not evaporated as I had thought. In fact, there was a little more than at first. This told me that there must be a tiny leak somewhere in the old skiff. It was nothing to worry about, but I kept my eye on it just the same.

Pickerel Lake is a beautiful spot, not quite as developed as Crooked Lake, thanks in large part to its remoteness and state land that covers most of the southwest shore. There is a large farm that covers the northwest corner of the lake, and on the remainder of the north side are many recently built fine cottages of various types. At the far east end of the lake is Camp Pet-O-Se-Ga, which loosely means "rising sun," a summer boys' camp that was established in the early thirties. And being mid-July and at the height of the summer camping season, the sounds of yells and laughter from the boys cascaded out over the water.

It was time for me to head back to the hotel and get freshened up for supper. This time, as I passed through the river and the Black Hole, I encountered several fishermen as well as some recreational boaters and paddlers. I waved and they waved back.

As I approached the dock at the hotel, I could see children, brown as walnuts from the sun, laughing and frolicking in the shallow water. Their parents were sitting in lounge chairs on the lawn or the sandy beach, reading paperbacks or napping. The old folks were sitting on the porch, or in the shade beneath the big oak. The women were wearing loose-fitting cotton dresses, and the men wore cotton short-sleeve shirts and wide-brimmed hats.

When I pulled up to moor, one of the children asked, "Hey Mister! Did you catch anything?" When I lifted my stringer full of fish out of the water, they squealed with delight.

I walked into the kitchen and Billy was still there, preparing for the evening meal. "Hey Billy, I've got something for you!" I held up the fish, still flopping, dripping on the kitchen floor. "Quick, get those in the sink! What am I supposed to do with these?" he asked.

"Put them on the menu," I said. "I can't do anything with 'em."

"The menu is already set for the next week," he said.

"Then they are yours. Get 'em into some ice and take them home."

"Thank you very much," Billy said, quickly putting the fish in a bucket and covering them with ice.

"What's for supper?" I asked.

"Your choice of fried chicken or smelt, with boiled corn on the cob and potato salad. This is the first of the Michigan sweet corn from down state. We'll start with a fruit cocktail and end with a scoop of vanilla ice cream topped with maple syrup."

"Chicken or smelt. Tough choice."

"I'll tell you what," said Billy. "I'll make sure you get some of each."

"You're too good to me, Billy!" I exclaimed.

Billy was a man of his word. When my plate arrived, it had a chicken thigh, a drumstick, and several smelts. I'm sure that the family from Cincinnati I was sharing a table with wondered why I was getting such special treatment, but not a word was said.

After supper, I strolled outside to enjoy the evening. I walked to the end of the porch and saw an older gentleman sitting by himself. "Mind if I join you?"

The white-haired man gestured to the empty wicker chair next to him. I sat down.

"I saw you come in from the water," the old man said. "Nice mess o' fish."

"Thanks. It was just a good day from start to finish. Billy fed me breakfast and packed a lunch for me. I know I'm a guest at the hotel, but he didn't have to do it. Then I just had a great day on the water. Caught some fish and some sunshine, and then I gave Billy my fish."

"Peaceful waters," the man said in a low voice.

"I beg your pardon?" I asked.

"Peaceful waters. That's what Pon-She-Wa-Ing means in the native tongue. That's what they called this place.""I couldn't agree more," I said. "It sure is peaceful."

"For me," the old man continued, "peaceful waters is more than just a place. It's a frame of mind. It's about being comfortable with who you are and the world you live in."

"I'm not sure I follow."

"Peaceful waters is about finding a certain balance in your life," he explained. "It's about being even-keeled, about not getting too worked up about the little stuff and not fretting too much over the big stuff. It's about being satisfied with who you are and what you have, rather than obsessing over the stuff you don't have. It's about treating people with kindness. It's all about the balance."

"I see."

"It took me a long time to find peaceful waters," the man continued. "Some people never find it. Too many people go through life bitter, or angry, or hateful, or jealous, or greedy and never find peaceful waters. Other people find peaceful waters at an early age, like Billy in the kitchen, and their lives are much richer for it. Billy, whether he realizes it or not, has discovered that kindness is fluid, it flows back and forth. He packed you a lunch. You gave him your fish, which I'm sure his family will enjoy very much. He didn't ask you if he could have your fish. You didn't ask him to pack you a lunch. Life on this earth is too short not to find peaceful waters."

A quietness came over the evening.

"Well," I said, "I think I'm going to walk the beach for a while and then turn in. It has been a long day, and I've got to put some ointment on this sunburn."

I started toward the water. Fireflies by the dozen were hovering over the lawn. The warm scent of lake water rose in the cooling air. I was about halfway across the lawn to the beach when the man called out, "Peaceful waters!"

I stopped, turned around, and smiled.

"Peaceful waters."

This story is fictitious, of course, but most of the details are accurate. On August 23, 1954, most of the Pon-She-Wa-Ing Hotel burned to the ground. Fortunately, the fire broke out during the day, and all guests safely exited the building. In June of 1968, the property was sold, and was developed for lakefront homes and cottages. The only remains of the Pon-She-Wa-Ing Hotel are the two stone pillars at the property entrance, still visible today from U.S. 31.

Lightning Bugs

who knows how or when
in the warm still evening dusk
fireflies make magic?

July 18

Embers, Fireflies & Stars

"Why don't you wait to put another log on the fire," I said.

"How come?" asked the boy.

"Let the fire die down a bit so we can get a better look at the stars."

It was a beautiful starlit night, cool, the kind of cool you feel after a hot summer day. The stars, the embers rising off the campfire, and the occasional firefly, created a magical environment.

"So, what are stars anyway?" the boy asked.

"They're like our sun, but much farther away."

"How far?"

"They are millions, billions, trillions of miles away," I explained, waving my arms a bit for theatrics. "Imagine if you were in a car traveling at sixty miles per hour. You would have to travel for a million years just to reach some of the nearest stars."

"I don't think I will live that long," the boy said with a laugh.

"Hardly. That's how big the universe is. And how small we are. In the universe, Earth is hardly a speck. We think our planet is a big place, but it's actually an incredibly tiny place. And it's the only place we have, so we better take care of it, and frankly, we're not doing a very good job of it."

July 20

Returning Home

in eve'ning distance
a lone truck on the highway
heard through screen window

August 5

The Lazy Rooster

heard distant rooster
it was about nine o'clock
must have slept in late

August 7

The First Sign of Fall

The first sign of fall is not what you think.
Not the evenings that begin to turn cold,
Nor the summer sun that starts to sink.
It's when the forest ferns turn gold.

Not when the maple leaf turns red,
Nor the return of the common cold,
Nor steel gray skies overhead.
It's when the forest ferns turn gold.

Not the end of motorboats at night,
Nor kids at school enrolled,
Nor when Canada geese take flight.
It's when the forest ferns turn gold.

August 11

FINN

Crickets & Cicadas

The summer songs of cicadas and crickets
Hiding, as they do, in grasses and thickets.
One buzzes at noon,
The other chirps to the moon,
They're August's concert sell-out tickets.

A cicada's song is reminiscent of
A tiny buzzsaw in the trees above.
And a cricket's white noise,
Is one of summer's sweet joys,
Yet both are mere languages of love.

August 14

Roadside Stand

sweet corn, tomatoes
fresh cukes, sweet cherries u-pick
up ahead on right

August 20

Hummingbirds

A bird is a bird, and a bee is a bee,
Yet a hummingbird sees things differently.

Birds can soar and birds can flap,
And bees are obsessed with nectar sap.

But a hummingbird operates under its own terms,
And lets bigger birds peck for earthly worms.

Like bees, hummingbirds prefer their nectar sweet,
And buzz around with nary a tweet.

They flit about from blossom to blossom,
With bee-like speed that seems nearly impossom.

They're just an oversized bee I've heard,
And sure glad that a bee is not as big as a bird.

August 20

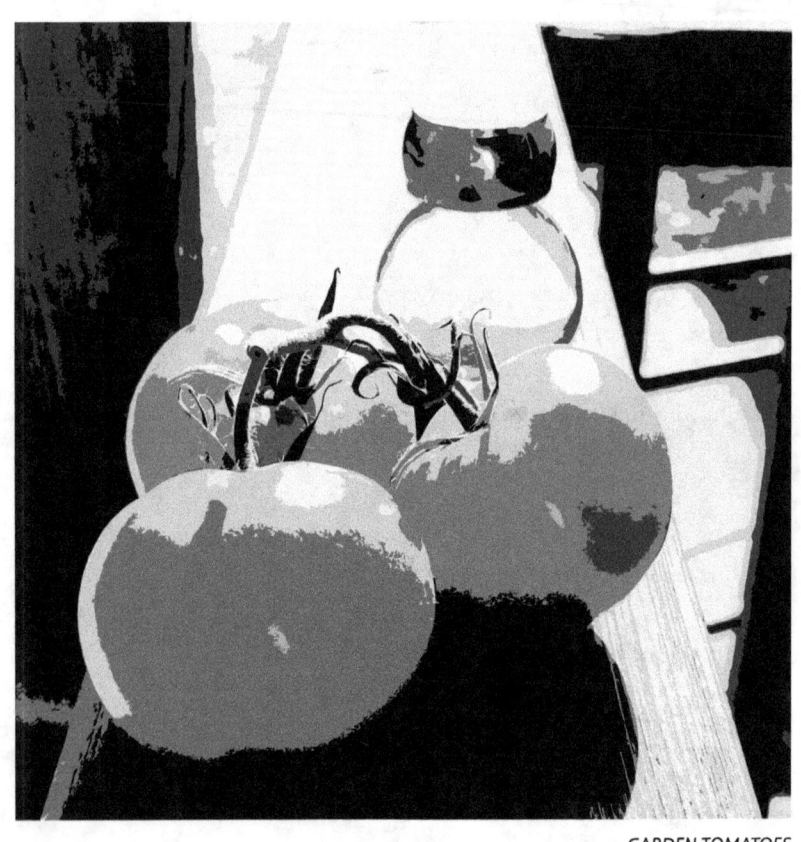

GARDEN TOMATOES

Garden Tomato

warm red and juicy
saltshaker in back pocket
chin wiped on a sleeve

August 23

Roadside Wildflowers

I've been thinking a lot about wildflowers these days. Mainly, I think, because the Queen Anne's lace is in full bloom. They are everywhere. And once you begin to notice Queen Anne's lace along the roadside, you also begin to notice yellow marsh marigolds, purple thistle, milkweed, coneflowers of various colors, black-eyed Susans, wild white daisies, and, of course, goldenrod.

Sumac has turned bright red. And, as if to catch up, a few maple leaves are already beginning to blush.

It's a glorious color palette that signals for me my favorite time of the year, the roughly six- or seven-week period from late August into early October. Warm days. Cool nights. Sweatshirts and sweaters.

No other period of the year is as brilliant. This is the time of year when Nature puts on her most colorful party dress and says, "Look at me!"

August 25

Fog

fog is but a cloud
hanging so close to the ground
just afraid of heights

September 15

STACKED DOCK AWAITING SPRING

Reflection on a Summer Past

boat turned upside down

oars and anchor tucked beneath

wood dock stacked nearby

September 22

OLD FRIENDS

Old Friends

rake with rusty tines
handle oiled by years of sweat
and old leather gloves

September 28

Apples, Books & People

Today, Tracy and I went to an apple festival in Charlevoix, and we bought a quarter-peck of apples to take home. We each ate one in the car. The apples were tasty, and we threw the cores into a field for the birds and deer to eat.

That apple got me to thinking, though.

I was reminded of an apple tree on the campus of Alma College. I discovered this tree, thankfully, my freshman year, and I looked forward to returning to it every fall.

It was a neglected apple tree, however, and the greenish yellow apples hanging from the branches were gnarly and deformed, every last one of them. On top of that, the bugs and birds had already feasted on most of them. Still, I could find a few untouched apples.

But here's the thing. Those apples were the best I've ever eaten. Just the right combination of tart and sweet; and really crisp – not at all like those mealy, tasteless, supermarket apples.

And when I bit into one, the juice would run down my chin, so that I'd have to wipe it on my sleeve. I'd try to find as many good ones as I could carry, using my sweatshirt as a basket, and I took them back to my dorm room. I never mentioned this apple tree to anyone. It was my secret.

Unfortunately, that apple tree is long gone, the victim of campus development.

Apples are a lot like books, you know. You can't judge a book by its cover, and you can't judge an apple by its appearance. And you can't get to know a person, either, until you see what's inside.

By the way, I sometimes think of that old apple tree and wonder. If the man on the bulldozer had just taken the time to bite into one of those gnarly, but juicy, supremely delicious apples, that tree might still be there today.

October 13

Fall Chores

Deck chairs and hoses were put in the shed.
The lawn mower, so sadly, was put off to bed.
The crawl space secured,
Winter warmth insured,
For the chill of the season ahead.

October 14

ROADSIDE CATTAILS

Cattails

A cattail is a swampy oddball,
Releasing its seeds in mid to late fall.
By the side of the road,
They abruptly explode,
Into a white cotton candy puff ball.

October 16

The First Sign of Winter

The first sign of winter is not what you think.
Not the furnace's attempt to take off the chill,
Nor plans for an ice skating rink.
It's when the last cricket goes still.

Not when a lone snowflake is seen,
Nor the closing of the cider mill,
Nor the coaxing of a snow-throw machine.
It's when the last cricket goes still.

Not the birdbath's icy freeze,
Nor a sled's track on the hill,
Nor the fresh coat of wax on skis.
It's when the last cricket goes still.

October 22

Autumn Heartbreak

summer has ended
lone cricket finding no love
ends his serenade

October 23

Work Ethic

corn stalks in dry rows
having fed both beast and man
boast to the fall wind

October 26

First Snow of the Season

Overnight, it snowed here about four inches. It weighed down the branches of the pines and the cedars.

The ground is too warm for the snow to last long. But it accumulated on the roofs of the barn and bird feeders.

October 31

At the Point of Freezing

a lone flake of snow
encouraged by charcoal skies
scolded by the rain

November 2

The Off-Season Player

idle lawn mower
having cut its chilly last
awaits spring training

November 5

Autumn

I think the best way to describe autumn is to say that it is a stew of emotions. Brilliant colors to start, then browns, and then mixed days of warm and cold. Leaves fall to earth, as will soon the snowflakes.

We have things pretty much buttoned up for winter. The leaves have, for the most part, been pushed off the lawn back into the woods, although I think I'll have one more opportunity to take care of the late-falling oak leaves if the weatherman is to be believed. All the outdoor furniture has been put in the barn.

Yesterday, I put yellow stakes along the driveway to guide me and the snow blower through winter. Tomorrow, I plan to dig out the seeds from our Hallowe'en pumpkin that has been sitting on our front porch and roast them in the oven.

Autumn is a time of reflection, to think back over the past year. Autumn is also a time to think ahead.

A time to think about spring and planting and warm earth.

A time to think about how the perennials we planted just a few weeks ago will survive the winter, and how beautiful they will be when they blossom next year.

A time to think about planting into paper cups the seeds I harvested from daisies and globe thistles and keeping them on the windowsill until seedlings appear.

A time to think about summer sun and laughter.

There is a particular sadness to autumn, as another year comes to an end. But there is also a sense of anticipation.

Who knows what next year will bring?

November 7

Deer Season

Two deer have taken refuge in our backyard,
They somehow know they will be safe there.
Still, they remain cautious and on guard,
For there is uncertainty in the air.

The older bucks have lived through this before,
When hunters await in the trees.
Gunshot echoes are hard to ignore,
As is human scent in the breeze.

So, they wait quietly behind our home,
And lie down among the ferns,
Until again it is safe to roam,
And the young buck once again learns.

November 15

APPLE HARVEST

Ode to the Michigan Apple

Florida has oranges and Georgia has peaches,
And California grows grapes not far from the beaches.

Wisconsin has cranberries in ruby red bogs;
Washington pears drop to earth like cats and like dogs.

And while Michigan grows a variety of fruit,
For me, the apple is our fruit absolute.

Cherry and grape folks, please do not fear,
Your respective fruits are simply without peer.

But the humble apple, especially in autumn,
Puts all other fruits, alas, at the bottom.

So many varieties, both common and auspicious,
Like Gala and Honeycrisp and Yellow Delicious.

There's Jonathan and McIntosh and Empire you see,
Braeburn and Cortland and even Fuji.

Apples eaten fresh from the side of the road,
Or in a warm apple pie, served, of course, *à la mode*.

Tart apple cider or cold apple juice,
Served as a sauce, or even a mousse!

Apples pair well with pork and with ham,
Or blended with sugar to make apple jam.

It's ideally minced inside sausage and wurst,
And a chilled appletini quenches a dry cocktail thirst.

Apples are ideal for strudeling and cobblering,
And perfectly suited for county fair bobbing.

Apples may be candied, baked, or sauteed,
And they make a tasty, barbequed rib marinade.

They can be sliced, diced, or eaten all whole,
Or found floating, politely, in a party punch bowl.

Apples are great in an ice cream parfait,
Or as a seasonal topping for a fine *crème brûlée*.

Apples can be mixed in a spiced coffee cake,
And literally anything else you can bake.

Apples appear in the Thanksgiving dressing,
And may also deserve mention in the tableside blessing!

Apples can star in a warm dessert crumble,
Perhaps the apple, after all . . . isn't so humble!

November 18

Conversation with a Fox

Cup of coffee in hand, I walked along the trail, alone, behind our house, to a quiet place to sit in the woods to enjoy the morning. And what a beautiful morning it was! The sun was shining through the trees, gradually taking the chill off the air. A fresh frost covered the moss on the trail.

I took a sip of my coffee, and when I lowered the cup to my lap, I saw a fox sitting across from me on the trail. A fox is generally wary of humans, and often nocturnal, so I was surprised that it was sitting there and not running off.

"Hi there, fella," I said cautiously. "What brings you here?"

"I just wanted to introduce myself to you," it said.

My coffee cup fell to the ground. "You, you, you can talk!" I stammered.

"Obviously. It's well known that foxes are smart."

"I've seen you often. You show up on our night vision camera."

"And I've been watching you, too. You see, I occasionally take a nap under your porch just outside your front door."

"Well, that explains why Finn is always sniffing under there," I said.

"Yes, Finn. She's a curious dog for sure. When I'm under the porch, I can see her big nose poke under there, but she can't see me. I must be careful. I'm not sure what Finn would do if we found ourselves face to face."

"She would probably chase you, I think, unless I told her to stay. Mostly, I think she would want to play with you," I said.

"I can't take chances. Dogs are unpredictable, you know."

"She's a great dog," I said in her defense. "She's really smart."

"I've seen her do tricks," the fox said. "Impressive. But that's really child's play you know."

"Child's play? What do you mean?" I asked.

"Well, a dog will do a trick for a reward, be it a treat or a pat on the head. But it's the rare dog that can survive by itself in the wild without human assistance."

"Oh, so that makes you so smart?" I challenged.

"Wisdom takes many forms. The greatest wisdom is knowing how to survive and to get along. Surviving in summer is not so difficult. Surviving in winter takes intelligence. Humans, if I may say so, have exhibited great intelligence as a species. As individuals, I think that very few have the intelligence to survive on their own."

"Oh really!"

"Think about it. What will you eat for dinner tonight if you can't go back to your refrigerator or you can't drive to the grocery store?"

"I'd find something to eat," I countered.

"What? What would you eat?" the fox questioned.

I paused. The fox was right. What would I eat? It might take days, or weeks, or months before I developed the knowledge and skills of how to eat on my own, especially in winter. "What do you eat?" I asked.

"I eat well," the fox said, "but I have to work at it. Mice are good. I'll eat berries and apples when they are in season. Rabbits and squirrels are very good. By the way, you have a lot of moles in your yard. Unfortunately, I don't much care for the taste of them."

"Too bad," I said. "They're making a mess of the lawn."

"If I feel brave," the fox continued, "I'll try to get a chicken at the farm on the other side of the woods. But that dog is mean, not like Finn. I know every inch of that farm, just like I know every inch of your house and yard. If the dog is distracted and a chicken gets careless, I'll have chicken for dinner."

"That sounds kind of cruel!"

"How is that any different than you bringing a chicken home from the grocery store?" the fox snapped. "The fate of the chicken is the same in either case."

"Wait. How do you know about grocery stores?"

"I said that foxes are smart, didn't I? We know everything about grocery stores. I prefer fresh food, but sometimes I'm forced to eat human leftovers. Humans waste an incredible amount of food, you know."

"Yeah, I know."

"I just wish the raccoons would leave some of the good stuff for the rest of us. Raccoons don't have good manners. And they really will eat anything. I'm more selective in what I eat."

"Speaking of raccoons," I said, "they show up on the night camera too, as well as 'possums, rabbits, deer, and skunks. How do you all get along?"

"We coexist," the fox replied. "We tend to give each other space. We recognize our individual differences, and we just generally try to get along. There's enough food in these woods for everyone. I must say, however, that I wish the skunks would move to another forest. They're not at all friendly, and . . . they smell!"

"I couldn't agree more!" I said.

"Yet, they deserve to be here as much as anyone. The only real problem is when coyotes wander through. They disrupt the balance."

There was a pause in the conversation. The fox lifted its nose and sniffed the air.

"What is it?" I asked.

"A porcupine, I think," the fox said. "I'm not sure. My nose isn't as good as my eyes or my ears. Did you know that I can hear a mouse squeak a hundred yards away?"

"Impressive."

There was another pause in the conversation, almost as if we were running out of things to say. "You're very smart. How old are you?" I asked.

"This is my fourth winter, so I guess that makes me four years old."

"You're very wise for being so young."

"I'm young by your standards," the fox explained, "but foxes only live three to five years, six if we're lucky."

"Oh, I'm sorry," I apologized.

"Sorry for what?" the fox said. "A lifetime is not measured in years, but in a life. I'm nearing the end of my life, and it has been a good life. You see, time is measured not in hours, or days, or years, but as a percentage of your life."

"What do you mean?"

The fox thought for a moment. "As you get older, time seems to pass more quickly, right? That's because any segment of time, say a year, becomes a smaller percentage of your total life experience. A year for you is a very small percentage of your life. But for me, a year is perhaps a quarter of my life. But here's the thing. I will experience just as much in a quarter of my life as you will in a quarter of yours."

"Interesting," I said.

The fox continued. "The real beauty of life is not the time of a life but the experience of a life. Make the most of your life, whether it is five years or eighty. Believe me, my five-year life will be every bit as fulfilling as whatever yours turns out to be."

I sat quiet for a moment, in awe of what I had just heard. "You know, I knew that foxes were smart, but I had no idea. So, tell me, why did you stop by to talk with me today?"

"It's quite simple really," said the fox. "You are new to the woods, and I would like us all to coexist."

I paused again. "Well, I think you will find us easy to get along with. Thanks for welcoming us to the neighborhood. Will we talk again?"

"Probably not," the fox said. "I think you've already received enough fox wisdom to last a lifetime."

"Yes, I believe I have. Is there anything else you'd like to say before you leave?"

"Yes," the fox said. "Can you try to keep Finn from sticking her nose under the porch?"

November 29

Forest Politics

Looked out my back window, and what did I see,
A black silhouette in front of the old poplar tree.

I was startled at first to see something so sizable,
But then instantly the figure became so recognizable.

A wild turkey it was, with some wild turkey friends;
A big ol' tom, and then eight turkey hens.

The tom forged ahead, all the more bold,
While the hens followed behind him in a manner controlled.

None of them seemed to be in much of a hurry,
Until something in the woods sent them off in a flurry.

What scared them off I was curious to know;
Then saw through the woods a buck and a doe.

A turkey does not scare a deer it appears,
An attack from a bird is not something it fears.

And I'm not quite sure what a deer might eat;
An apple, perhaps, but not turkey meat.

Animals get along if they share the same foe,
A fact that even politicians very well know.

Turkey and deer get along for that very same reason;
Because Thanksgiving coincides with deer hunting season.

December 3

WINTER BEACH, LAKE MICHIGAN

Hikes & Walks

All hikes are walks some will suggest,
But all walks are not hikes I can surely attest.

The dictionary says they are one and the same.
The same activity, yet with a different name.

A walk can take place almost anywhere,
On the street, the beach, or the county fair.

A walk can meander to and fro,
With no particular place to go.

But a hike has purpose and an expectation,
And requires a tad bit of navigation.

A hike is a walk with a much longer distance,
And with a specified destination, for instance.

Even if your hike is a circuitous route,
There still is an ending point, without a doubt.

A hike often requires special clothing and shoes,
Whereas on a walk you can wear whatever you choose.

A walk might get you from Point A to Point B,
But a hike takes a walk to a higher degree!

December 18

Shortest Day of the Year

Winter solstice is the shortest day of the year,
But it does bring with it a slight bit of cheer.

It's the beginning of winter with winds that are stronger,
But now the days will only get longer.

The day also brings occasional grins,
Knowing that, for those down under, summer begins.

December 21

Finn

A dog, as they say, is man's best friend,
And no truer words ever were penned.

There are dogs that hunt and dogs that play,
And dogs that sleep away the day.

But Finn lives to be happy at our side.
A dog's life lived most satisfied.

She barks too much when there are strangers,
Protecting us from "potential dangers."

But she's just performing her job you see,
Doing what's required of her pedigree.

They say no poem's as lovely as a tree,
Nor of a dog, a friend, most faithfully.

December 24

FINN ON BURT LAKE ICE

Epilogue

Tracy and I, along with Finn, took a walk today at Burt Lake State Park in Indian River, partly to get some exercise and partly to check out some possible campsites for summer camping. The park is open to winter hikers, but the campground area is closed to automobile traffic, so we parked in the designated lot and hiked through the woods to the campground.

We were all alone. There were no other cars or people to be seen, which seemed a bit odd being that this was New Year's Eve. In comparison, a few days ago, we walked the beach at Petoskey State Park and there were a good number of cars parked there and quite a few people at the beach. There was no snow on the ground that day, which is a rarity for late December, so it was quite unusual to walk on a sandy beach this time of year. We had Finn on a leash, primarily to keep her out of the water and not covered in wet sand.

But today it was snowing, and the snow would accumulate on Finn's back, so that we would have to occasionally brush her off. Despite the signs that read, "Even Good Dogs Need to Be Leashed," we let Finn run free because we were all alone. She never got too far ahead of us, and she continually looked behind to make sure we were still there. When we got to the water's edge, Finn stepped into the water half-way up her legs. She would have gone all the way in had we not stopped her. Taking care of a wet dog on a sub-freezing day is not something we wanted to deal with and Finn, thankfully, obeyed.

Aside from the sound of our boots in the snow, it was eerily silent, a sharp contrast to what the campground is like during the summer months: the laughter of kids riding bikes, or playing in the water, dogs barking, the sound of motorboats out on the lake, and people conversing around the campfire. In the summer, the evening air would be thick with campfire smoke, but today the air was fresh and cold. All the campfire pits have long gone cold and the picnic tables were tilted on their sides.

In summer, there would literally be hundreds of camping trailers, motorhomes, and tents, with the accompanying vehicles, but today we could look at the campground uninterrupted from one end to the other.

The stark contrast between winter and summer made me think of the year I had just chronicled in verse.

Northern Michigan winters are long, nearly half the year. Summers are always too short it seems. Spring and fall are indeed short, and it feels like winter turns into summer, and summer turns into winter, with hardly a blink of an eye.

But the changing of the seasons is something to behold. The changes can't be seen daily, but rather weekly, when you can say to yourself, "Yes, things are a little different than they were a week ago." There is a constant push-pull between the seasons, as if the outgoing season is reluctant to let go.

In winter, shoveling snow is a daily routine, and even on the days it doesn't snow, it seems that we are still managing it in some way. Personally, I don't mind the cold, and it has to get below zero degrees before I start to complain.

Spring brings with it the welcomed smell of the earth and the color green. It is every bit a rebirth with a heightened anticipation of the weeks and months that lie ahead.

Northern Michigan summers are simply magnificent in so many ways. Sun on your face. The smell of newly mowed grass and the sounds of nature at every turn.

Fall is the most pleasant for me, with still-warm days and cooler nights, when nature is at its most colorful, with fire pits, apples, and fresh food markets where farmers can proudly show off their summer labor.

We've become acquainted with a wide range of critters in our very own yard: foxes, deer, rabbits, opossums, skunks, wild turkeys, mice, moles, and squirrels. We've seen bald eagles fly overhead, heard woodpeckers, crows, and robins echo through the woods, and had humming-birds fly so close that we could touch them if they would let us.

We've enjoyed the tug of a bass or bluegill at the end of our spinning rod.

We've enjoyed snowflakes in the woods and sunsets at the beach.

We've enjoyed our many flower gardens, those we inherited and those we planted ourselves.

And we have enjoyed meeting so many genuinely nice people, some of them neighbors, while others we have met at the local hardware store, grocery, bait & tackle shop, or restaurant. We have met friendly folks at fairs, festivals, and farmers markets.

But today, as the snow fell around us at Burt Lake, the year seemed perfectly complete. On the way home, we stopped at one of Northern Michigan's many wineries, and Tracy and I each enjoyed a hot spiced wine, featuring one of the locally grown reds flavored with citrus, cin-namon, and cloves. It was a most fitting way to warm ourselves after a cold walk in the woods and to celebrate our first full year of living in our little nest in the universe.

December 31

About the Author

Jeff Leestma is a retired communications executive in the automotive industry. He has served as president of the Automotive Hall of Fame and managing editor of *Automobile Quarterly*. He is the author of *COPO Camaro: The Chevrolet Performance Team Unleashes a Legend* (Automobile Heritage Publishing, 2012, USA), and a contributing writer to *Dodge: America's Most Emotional Car Brand for More Than 90 Years* (Juergen Zoellter, Delius Klasing Verlag, 2006, Germany).

He is a graduate of Alma College (Alma, Michigan) with a degree in English.